from the author

The Gender Book
Girls, Boys, Non-Binary, and Beyond
Cassandra Jules Corrigan
Illustrated by Jem Milton
ISBN 978 1 83997 710 7
eISBN 978 1 83997 711 4

The Pronoun Book
She, He, They, and Me!
Cassandra Jules Corrigan
Illustrated by Jem Milton
ISBN 978 1 78775 957 2
eISBN 978 1 78775 958 9

of related interest

Who Are You?
The Kid's Guide to Gender Identity
Brook Pessin-Whedbee
Illustrated by Naomi Bardoff
ISBN 978 1 78592 728 7
eISBN 978 1 78450 580 6

MY CULTURE, MY GENDER, ME

Cassandra Jules Corrigan

Illustrated by Moe Butterfly

Jessica Kingsley Publishers
London and Philadelphia

First published in Great Britain in 2024 by Jessica Kingsley Publishers
An imprint of John Murray Press

1

Copyright © Cassandra Jules Corrigan 2024

The right of Cassandra Jules Corrigan to be identified as the Author of
the Work has been asserted by them in accordance with the Copyright,
Designs and Patents Act 1988.

Illustrations copyright © Moe Butterfly 2024
Front cover illustration source: Moe Butterfly.

A CIP catalogue record for this title is available from the British Library
and the Library of Congress

ISBN 978 1 83997 762 6
eISBN 978 1 83997 763 3

Printed and bound in China by Leo Paper Products Ltd

Jessica Kingsley Publishers' policy is to use papers that are natural,
renewable and recyclable products and made from wood grown in
sustainable forests. The logging and manufacturing processes are expected
to conform to the environmental regulations of the country of origin.

Jessica Kingsley Publishers
Carmelite House
50 Victoria Embankment
London EC4Y 0DZ

www.jkp.com

John Murray Press
Part of Hodder & Stoughton Limited
An Hachette UK Company

To Hinaleimoana Wong-Kalu and Yuhki Kamatani,

two real life visionaries who inspire greatness in us all.

Hello, my name is Alawa. I am Nêhiyaw, from the Moosomin First Nation in Canada.

When you look at me, which gender do you see? Many people would assume that I am either a girl or a boy (female or male).

However, many people do not fit into the definitions of male or female, and instead identify as one of many non-binary genders.

You may be familiar with some common non-binary genders, such as genderqueer, genderfluid, or bigender, but did you know that many cultures around the world have different genders specific to them?

10

For example, I identify as Two Spirit, an umbrella term used to describe a variety of gender identities specific to Indigenous tribes across North America. Prior to colonization, over 150 Native American tribes recognized some type of third gender outside of the gender binary.

Let me introduce you to some of my friends from around the world!

12

My name is Alohilani. I am a māhū person from Hawaii.

I embody both the femininity and masculinity that exists in each of us. For many years, my gender was stigmatized, but by living openly as a māhū, I can help preserve my native Polynesian culture.

14

My name is Nayeli. I am from Oaxaca in Mexico and I was assigned male at birth, but I am now a muxe.

Being a muxe means different things to everyone— some of us identify as gender non-conforming men, while others see themselves as trans women, or as a third gender altogether.

16

I am Ilhan and this is my friend Ishrat. I was born in India but raised in Pakistan. I am a hijra—not quite man or woman.

I am part of a rich community of people fighting for inclusion and gender equality.

18

My name is Chideziri. I am a female husband from Nigeria, and I come from the Igbo people.

I was assigned female at birth, but I take on the roles and responsibilities of a man in my marriage to my wife. For example, I am able to partake in the breaking of Ójì (otherwise known as kola nuts), a sacred showing of respect in my culture, usually completed by men. And yet my femininity is not forgotten; it is celebrated.

20

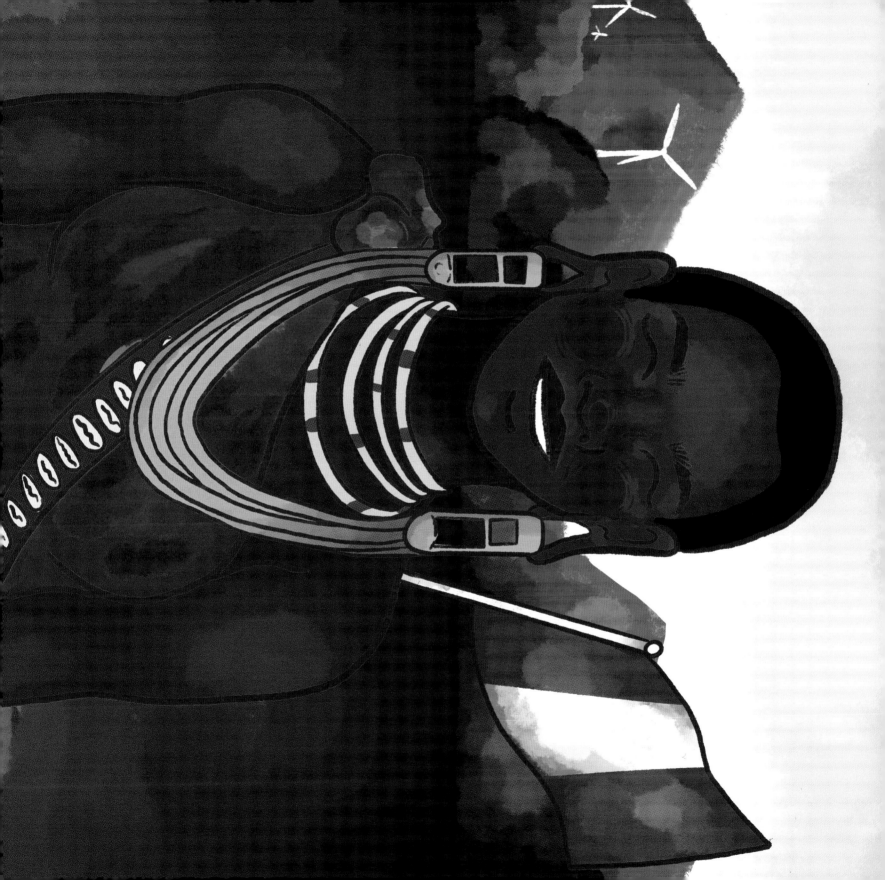

My name is Rabbi Aaron Huber. From my study of the Talmud, I have learned that ancient Jewish law lists as many as eight different genders.

I hope that by sharing this information I can broaden the minds of everyone—Jewish and gentile (non-Jewish) alike.

22

My name is Kohei and I'm X-gender. In Japan, X-gender is an umbrella term that's similar to non-binary. There are many subcategories that X-gender people fall into.

As for me, I don't aspire to label myself with one of the subcategories—I only hope that by following my dream of creating manga with X-gender characters I can help younger trans people across Japan feel accepted.

24

Our names are Dalla and Ithu. Where we live in Australia, some Aboriginal people who were assigned male at birth and identify more strongly with femininity are called sistergirls.

26

My name is Andi, and I'm from Indonesia. I come from an ethnic group called the Bugis, who recognize five distinct genders that must all live in harmony.

My role is that of a bissu, meaning I carry aspects from all genders.

Hello, my name is Aishatu, and I am one of many 'yan daudu of the Hausa people of Sub-Saharan Africa—a 'dan daudu.

Much like the muxe in Mexico, 'yan daudu has different meanings to different people. But to me, being a 'dan daudu means being assigned male at birth but transcending the categories of male and female entirely.

Hello, my name is Dakila, and I live in the Philippines. I identify as a baklâ, a gender identity that has been recognized in my country for centuries.

Today, baklâs form an incredible subculture—we have pageants, celebrations, and even our own language!

Ciao! I'm Caterina from Napoli, Italy, but you probably know my hometown better as Naples! I am a femminiello—a transfeminine person.

In my town, femminiello are not shunned for our gender; instead we are thought to bring good luck. Often, new parents bring children, like Marco, to me to hold, in hopes that my good fortune will rub off on them.

36

Hello, my name is Thiri, and I live in Myanmar. I am an acault, or a person who was assigned male at birth but exhibits feminine traits.

In my culture, many people are animists, meaning they believe in spirit gods called nats. One of these nats is called Manguedon—a female spirit who is thought to bless acaults like me with our femininity.

38

Author's note

Firstly, I am a white American, and although my editors and I have tried our best to research and present these cultural topics with care, we may have made some mistakes!

Secondly, some characters draw inspiration from real people. I hope I have done service in portraying these genders for younger Western audiences.

Finally, I want to thank you all for reading my writing and books like mine that showcase identities and histories that aren't always taught in school.

Cultural gender identities activity

Step one: Talk to an adult about your heritage. This adult could be a parent, a guardian, or an older family member such as a sibling, aunt or uncle, or grandparent.

If you can't talk to your biological family, you could also ask a teacher or librarian to help you learn about your culture—they may be able to narrow down your cultural background based on your last name.

Try to find out what your ethnicity and nationality are. For this activity, we'll mostly be interested in your ethnicity.

Sometimes, your ethnicity and nationality are one and the same. For example, if you live in the United Kingdom, your ethnicity and nationality might both be English.

For other people, your ethnicity and nationality may be very different. For example, your nationality could be Irish, but your ethnicity could be Kikuyu, or your nationality could be American, while your ethnicity could be Polish.

Step two: With an adult's help, use the internet or library catalog to see if your ethnic group has any specific gender identities. Search terms like "transgender identities in different cultures" and "third gender cultures" are good starting points.

Step three: Try to find lists or articles that break down different identities from each region or country.

Step four: Look for your culture and see if anything is mentioned.

Step five: If you aren't having any luck, return to your search. Try searching "gender in ancient [insert country or region]" or "gender in ancient [ethnic group] communities."

Step six: If you still can't find anything, that's okay! Not all cultures have specific gender identities to find. Do you have any friends of different cultures that you would like to learn about instead?

Cultural gender identities map

Can you match the cultural gender identities listed below with the part of the world they come from? Fill in the labels on the map opposite.

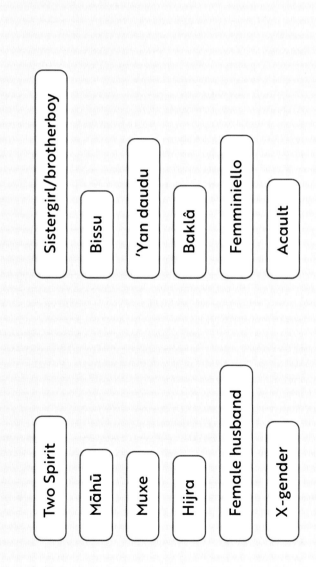

Two Spirit

Māhū

Muxe

Hijra

Female husband

X-gender

Sistergirl/brotherboy

Bissu

'Yan daudu

Baklâ

Femminiello

Acault

44